WELCOME TO "AQUATIC WONDERS: A COLORING BOOK"

DIVE INTO THE FASCINATING WORLD OF THE OCEANS AND DISCOVER THE BEAUTY OF ITS INHABITANTS WITH "AQUATIC WONDERS"! THIS COLORING BOOK INVITES YOU TO EXPLORE THE RICH DIVERSITY OF MARINE LIFE THROUGH CAPTIVATING ILLUSTRATIONS.

READY TO EMBARK ON A JOURNEY OF COLOR AND DISCOVERY? DIVE INTO THE PAGES OF "AQUATIC WONDERS" AND LET THE MAGIC OF THE OCEANS COME TO LIFE UNDER YOUR HANDS!

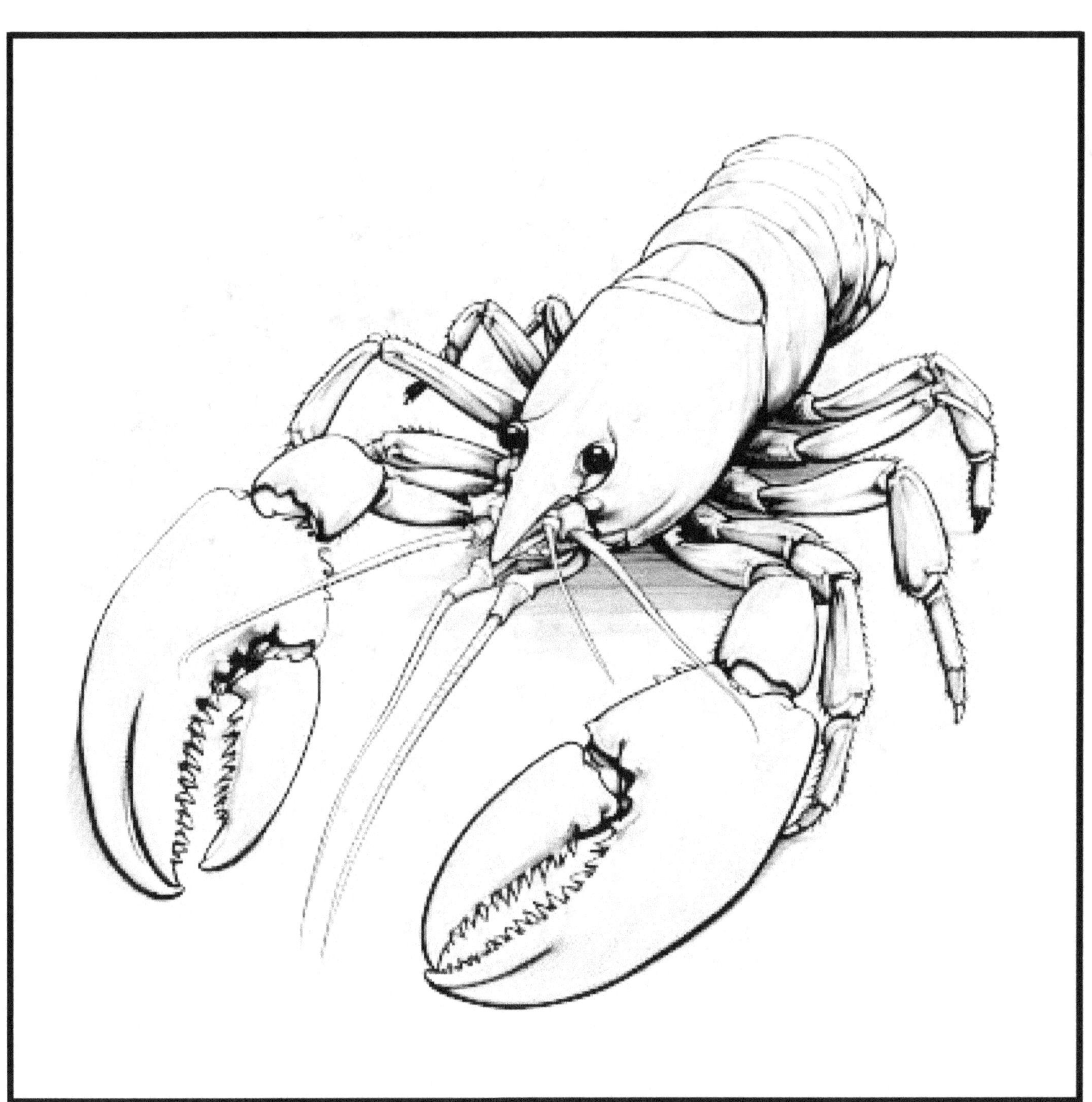

www.ingramcontent.com/pod-product-compliance
Lightning Source LLC
Chambersburg PA
CBHW081021260726
48662CB00025B/2634